THIS ISN'T THE
FOOTBALL FIELD!

and other pieces of my Puzzled Life!

IMA C. TOOITT

WESTBOW
PRESS®
A DIVISION OF THOMAS NELSON
& ZONDERVAN

This book is a work of non-fiction. Unless otherwise noted, the author and the publisher make no explicit guarantees as to the accuracy of the information contained in this book and in some cases, names of people and places have been altered to protect their privacy.

WestBow Press books may be ordered through booksellers or by contacting:

WestBow Press
A Division of Thomas Nelson & Zondervan
1663 Liberty Drive
Bloomington, IN 47403
www.westbowpress.com
844-714-3454

Because of the dynamic nature of the Internet, any web addresses or links contained in this book may have changed since publication and may no longer be valid. The views expressed in this work are solely those of the author and do not necessarily reflect the views of the publisher, and the publisher hereby disclaims any responsibility for them.

Any people depicted in stock imagery provided by Getty Images are models, and such images are being used for illustrative purposes only. Certain stock imagery © Getty Images.

Scriptures taken from the Holy Bible, New International Version®, NIV®. Copyright © 1973, 1978, 1984, 2011 by Biblica, Inc.™ Used by permission of Zondervan. All rights reserved worldwide. www.zondervan.com The "NIV" and "New International Version" are trademarks registered in the United States Patent and Trademark Office by Biblica, Inc.®

ISBN: 979-8-3850-1133-9 (sc)
ISBN: 979-8-3850-1134-6 (e)

Library of Congress Control Number: 2023920802

Print information available on the last page.

WestBow Press rev. date: 11/14/2023

Contents

Puzzles

PUZZLES OF ANY KIND HAVE always been a big part of my life. Any kind of puzzles: word, jigsaw, sudoku, crossword, or even a math problem has always captured my attention. One of my favorites is a tangled mess of necklaces. I have always enjoyed the challenge to get them straightened out or to complete or finish any other kind of enigma.

From my childhood, I remember my mother enjoying putting together a complex jigsaw puzzle, only to put it back in the box to solve again another day. That was the part that I hated. Taking apart what she had completed with what had started as a mess only to turn it back into a jumbled mix of pieces in a box was frustrating to me. Once I get something done, why would I want to do the same thing all over again?

The ingenuity of gluing puzzles together was absolutely genius. Credit of great magnitude should go to that amazing inventor. Glued together jigsaw puzzles are a beautiful reminder that something that was once a mess can be carefully and patiently put back together, sealed with the permanence of glue and allowed to display the work and diligence of the puzzle master.

In many ways my life has been a puzzle, a confusing mess that did not seem to have a solution; the pieces not fitting anywhere I tried to place them. It wasn't until 1988 that I that I put my hands up in surrender (no, I wasn't arrested!). Humbly, I fell on my knees and begged God to forgive me and please take over my life that had been like one of Mom's old puzzles in the attic—put together, taken apart many times only to be thrown out in a tattered box with lost and broken pieces.

Broken, sad, and relieved, I gave my life to God that Sunday morning in that sales meeting bonus time with our speaker. Crying out to God was the best choice in finding what my life needed.

The best part of that day is that it was just the beginning. Every day since has been like a new start. Each day has had its own challenges or trials, but there has always been hope that even though each situation would not always be solved or completed by the end of the day, the Master is not finished. There is still more work to be done to take a shaken box of broken pieces and to create the work of art that has become my life.

Just as my children and I enjoy the many glued puzzles decorating our homes, may you enjoy these stories of faith, fun, and encouragement as a gift from the Master of my life, the Lord Jesus Christ. Be encouraged. God has a plan for your life. God's word to the prophet Jeremiah to be written for all generations, including today with all of our trials and hardships states, "'For I know the plans I have for you,' declares the Lord, 'plans to prosper you and not to harm you, plans to give you hope and a future.'" Jeremiah 29:11, but there is a caveat in verse 12. Maybe you should look that one up.

Memories

IT HAS BEEN ON MY heart for a long time to compile the stories of encouragement and faith that have never faded from my memories. My childhood did not occur in what I would have considered to be a Christian home as I know what that means to me now. My folks were hard working plain people who loved their families and gathered together with as many as we could as often as possible.

Just being a member of my mom and dad's families was like being a piece in a great puzzle! Mom was the youngest of 6, 4 girls and 2 boys. Dad was one of 16 children, 9 boys and 7 girls and they loved their parents and siblings very much. Trying to remember all of my aunts, uncles and cousins names was like trying to memorize the books of the Bible. I didn't know all of them very well, but we visited them often. People visited each other more frequently then. Telephone calls were expensive because each township only had a small telephone company so every call had a fee, no plans. So we would take a drive and see who was home. We always found someone from all of those families who was available and looking forward to having visitors. Investing in our lives is what they were doing, and

I didn't realize that until I was older. So many of the things I have enjoyed doing have come as a result of visiting friends and family.

My folks expected us to go to church, but we mostly went with neighbors or friends. Mom went sometimes, but Dad rarely did. It was a small town country church that was called a federated church since the Baptists and Presbyterians agreed to congregate together. I learned a lot about the love of God and about the stories from the Bible, but salvation was not a clear part of that education. The basic belief was that you tried to be good, and somehow attending church was important to your reputation in the community.

However, it was fun to go to church. There were many ladies who taught me all kinds of things. Some of the loveliest and kindest women I would ever meet I met in that little church. I learned about gardening, woodworking, painting, and teaching. They encouraged me, and I got to eventually teach Sunday school and Vacation Bible School. Teaching became a passion for me, and I have come to realize it is a gift from God to teach. He has given me that gift and fulfilled so many of the desires of my heart by allowing me to teach. Opportunities to teach math, painting, paper-crafting, business courses, and Bible classes have been some of the most fulfilling roles God has given me.

In a way by documenting all of the many lessons in my life, I am hoping to teach and inspire others that God has a plan for their lives. No matter how it starts, life is filled with opportunities to enjoy the brief journey on planet earth.

The verses in Jeremiah 29 have become a promise to me. God does have a plan and nothing is meant to harm me but rather to make me stronger in my faith in Him as long as I seek HIM with my whole heart. Pause often and think of the people who have poured their life lessons into you. Being thankful for all of those people is so much better than focusing on the few that have hurt us.

Forgiveness

THE STORY OF JOSEPH FROM the book of Genesis in the Bible is probably the one story that has taught me about life, no matter what I was going through. Joseph seemed like an innocent enough kid who just knew his father loved him, and he loved and wanted to be loved by his brothers. Just as things didn't go as Joseph probably had planned, things do not always go as we think they will either.

Growing up as a girl in a home filled with gruff, tough manly men was often frustrating. "You can't do that; you're a girl." Now, hear me; being a feminist was not my goal. It was all about my father being proud of me, too, so that he could see that I could do things just as well as his sons. It didn't always work, especially during the time in my youth came when the boys at school began to notice me.

Dad was strict. I am convinced that he thought no one would ever be good enough for me. Some of the nicest guys even approached my dad and asked with much humility and fear if they could take me on a date. The resounding "No" from my father scared most of them away. So I was left only to be allowed to see men who were much older than I, and somehow that seemed to work for Dad. He could enjoy a conversation and then send me on my way with any stranger many years older than I was.

One of the very first times Dad agreed to let me go was when I was fifteen. The young man was over twenty, but because he was a military man, that made him right in Dad's eyes. It occurred to me that my date thought I was much older than fifteen, but what girl corrects a guy at that age. I didn't.

Do you ever go back and hit the replay button about events in your life and wonder if you had done something differently would the results have had a better outcome? Of course, this is one of those events. Perhaps had I told him my real age and been truthful, he would have behaved differently. But he took me somewhere and did things that I begged him not to and said "No," but he did what he wanted without regard to tears and fear. He dropped me home, and I never heard from him again. Many years later it was defined as "date rape," but I could never tell anyone until decades after.

Being treated like a throw away became the theme of my puzzled young life. I believed no one could ever really love me, not even GOD. No one would want a broken version of an innocent, naïve, and foolish girl.

My dad would never know, but he gave me to the wolves that night. He hadn't really protected me. He wasn't seeking to know the character of the men. The biggest rejection was not what this man had done, but what my father didn't do. I believed my own father didn't love me. That was the beginning of a long, broken cycle of trust in the male figures in my life. This caused bad decision making for more than a decade. I even wondered how God could love me.

However, on that Sunday morning in July 1988, understanding God's unconditional love for me and accepting Christ as my Savior allowed me to see the power of forgiving these men in my life. Forgiving my dad for his role in all of it was powerful. Finding the strength to forgive that man was the most liberating for me. It is my hope and prayer that he also came to know Christ and know he truly is forgiven. I forgave those who influenced me into giving up my dreams. I pray that they all have come to a personal relationship with Christ. Sometimes people who hurt us emotionally are harder to forgive than those who physically hurt us, but I am reminded by the words of Joseph, "You intended to harm me, but God intended it for good to accomplish what is now being done, the saving of many lives" Genesis 50:20. What Joseph's enemies meant for evil, God used for good.

Selfishness seeks only to do that which is good for oneself. Humility is walking away when it is not part of God's plan, and finding a way to be at peace with those moments we think will never be offered to us again.

The reconciliation with my Father in heaven and my dad on earth were some of the sweetest memories in my life. When I was twenty-four, God opened my heart, and I rose from my seat to go forward to publicly recognize Him as my Lord. That moment was as wonderful as my dad telling me he loved me and was proud of me, which did not occur until I was over thirty years old. Enduring hardship was what my dad watched me accomplish, not receiving awards or being elected to positions of greatness. It was the grind of hardship and putting the pieces of my shattered life back together that pleased my dad. The Bible tells us that is what pleases our heavenly Father. "Endure hardship with us like a good soldier of Christ Jesus" 2 Timothy 2:3.

Bitterness

HOW DOES A PIECE OF the root left behind from a tooth that was pulled over thirty-two years before teach us anything? This is a good analogy to the idea of a "root of bitterness" that the Bible talks about. Just as God's word teaches that we must surrender that bitter root to Him, when we surrender our lives in every aspect to God, everything in our lives can/will be used by Him.

There was an event in my life that seemed to be the point of regret for everything bad that happened in my life. It was one of those moments we tell ourselves, "I put others before myself; therefore, it must have been the right thing to do."

When a piece of tooth left behind suddenly decided it wanted out, an action had to be taken. The pain was overwhelming, but I really didn't know what was causing the pain until I sought the wisdom of a professional. He told me what this little piece of tooth was doing after all those years. The bone fragment was causing irritation. No kidding. Irritation! I could tell you I was irritated because my mouth hurt constantly, but inwardly I asked whom was I irritated with? The dentist who originally pulled my painfully abscessed tooth? My parents who had not gotten me regular dental checkups? Why not be irritated with everyone I ever knew—surely somehow this pain was the result of someone else's wrong doing!

God is so much bigger than the pain we will ever bear here on earth. I began to realize what I was feeling was literally a root of bitterness. Ephesians 4:31 is very clear about ridding ourselves of bitterness. But to rid ourselves of bitterness, we must understand what it is.

It is defined as "a feeling of deep and bitter anger and ill will; a taste that is unpleasant." Anger and ill will—could it be that I was now mad at these people for my current uncomfortable circumstances? How was this going to make the pain go away?

God allowed many of His servants to be placed in circumstances that were out of their comfort zones. Joseph was sold by his brothers to be a slave. That had to be uncomfortable to say the least. But later he was used by God to save his people. A beautiful girl named Esther, whose people were not in the king's favor, became the wife of the king. This obviously also was not a comfortable situation, but because of her decision, she was able to save her people later. Paul was placed in prison for teaching about Jesus. Yet the letters he wrote during his imprisonment are still used by God to minister to His people every day.

How does any of this relate to a toothache? Recognizing that this "new" ache was the result of a piece of root left in my mouth and the significance of a root of bitterness, I began to wrestle with God. So, it was wrong to be angry with a dentist who cared for me over thirty years ago. (By the way, the moment he pulled that tooth, I had such immediate relief that I think I may have worshipped him a little.)

How could I ever blame my parents? I know they always tried

their best with the resources they had. I love and miss them both so very much, and it grieves me to want to blame them for anything.

What I realized was that when one has tooth pain, looking in the mirror becomes a frequent event. I kept looking to see if my face were as huge as it felt. As God often does, He caused me to realize the person He was working on was looking right back at me. He wanted me to rid myself of that feeling of deep anger and ill will toward some folks who really didn't deserve it.

Oh, man, this was really a spiritual lesson to go with all of the physical pain! Indeed, God is still working on me. I am like that craft project that is never really completed.

Remember. I told you there was an event I had experienced that I kind of blamed for all of the failed events in my life. Well, this is really the situation where God wanted to do the work in my life. Deep down inside, I was angry that because a certain individual reacted a particular way, the teacher who oversaw/mentored both of us didn't know what to do. One individual was crying and inconsolable because her dream would not come true. The other was confident that no matter what the names on the ballots were, the best candidate would get the job.

That was until the teacher threw a wrench into the situation. What if one of the people stepped down? The inconsolable one with tears and emotions would not give in. The one who believed the best one would win gave in—and without even trying!

I'll bet you thought I was the one in tears! Nope, I stepped away from one of the moments that has defined my life. I gave in to make sure someone else was happy. I would rather endure the heartbreak than know that I caused someone else to be defeated.

Had this little piece of irritating tooth caused me to realize the bitterness I had harbored all these years? Paul writes in Ephesians 4:31 to all of those believers, "Get rid of all bitterness, rage, and anger brawling and slander along with every form of malice." And I thought it was just a little root of an old tooth I needed to get rid of.

Teenagers don't always make decisions based on what the consequences of their actions will be thirty years down the road. Well, I never considered that stepping down and not running for that coveted opportunity would affect my soul for those so many years. My childhood friend meant more to me than the opportunity. Her tears were the catalyst for a decision that caused pain to me for the rest of my life.

Writing the what-if chapters of my life from that pivotal moment seemed to make the grass oh so much greener on the other side of the hill—had my decision to remain in the race been different. What if I had won and had the privilege to be the one to travel the state, speaking and encouraging other young people? What if I had had the opportunity to attend all of the leadership training that was a reward for winning the election? What if I had learned to have more self-confidence in my decisions?

This tooth was causing me to reflect on the inward source of my pain and bitterness. The choice was made over thirty years before so why had I not just accepted the consequences? Who does want to accept consequences? God was still working on me with the life I had begun that day in 1988 when making the decision to be a Christ follower. Anything before that is done…forgiven…pulled out! Any remnants of the bitterness had found a way to cause an irritation that proved these things need to be gone.

Well, the dentist worked on the piece of root for almost two and half hours in the office, and he couldn't get it all! After all that effort, and a remnant was still left behind! For the next six weeks, my mouth was so sore from all of the work, but the healing process was taking over, creating new where the old had been traumatized. As that healing took place, it was in those weeks that my heart understood there was no one to be bitter with about anything. My life was a result of decisions I had made; no one had forced me. I was the owner of the consequences of my own choices. This was so mentally healing. Peace as I had never known was now a part of my innermost being.

The best part of all this as God used this stubborn little piece of root to teach me a much bigger life lesson was that as quickly as the pain began, it left one day. I was driving somewhere one day, and I felt something poking through my gum. I stopped the car and pulled on the protrusion in my gum. Six weeks after the dentist had tried for hours to extract this little piece of bone, it came out effortlessly. I sat holding this little root of a tooth that a professional could not extract and realized that when we let something go, God will remove it forever. Being delivered from the stronghold of bitterness was liberating and so was losing that old tooth root!

Wedding Day

THE JOY OF GETTING MARRIED is often complicated by a lot of planning and preparing. So many young women make the mistake of focusing on the celebration of the wedding and not the lifetime of the marriage. That was certainly the case for me. I was excited about getting married, which would include moving out of my home state. Looking back, I wonder if it was actually the prospect of living in North Carolina that was the bigger goal.

Of course, the ceremony would take place in the church, but neither my fiancé nor I would truly invite God into our marriage. The picture in my mind of a pastel rainbow wedding represented my dream. There was no question that my maid of honor was going to be my sister. She is my only sister and though she is younger than I, no one on this earth understood being a girl growing up in our caveman style mentality household better than she did. However, because we had our own distinct personalities, we reacted totally differently to the environment. I became a people pleaser, trying to make everyone happy while internally I was miserable. She was the beautiful sister who was vivacious and courageous. I still admire her to this day. She was the light and joy throughout this entire process of my getting married. Although she was barely fifteen when all of this was going on, she was the happiness and fun in all of it.

The bridesmaids were an array of those who had encouraged me through that difficult year after high school. There is a story to tell regarding that, but it deserves its own few pages. There were three very unique friends that, as I think back, were an incredible group of women from totally different backgrounds who inspired moments of deep encouragement in my life. Those moments were the reason I chose them as part of my bridal party. There were also my fiancé's sisters. Not only did I love those girls then, but I still love them today. To me, they became my little sisters when I joined his family. And then the highlights of my life were my nieces. They were adorable. At the time, the youngest one was less than 2. Her parents thought she was too young to participate, so my sweet and beautiful older nieces got to be my flower girls.

Oh, thinking of all those details in the wedding preparation was mind boggling, including handmade dresses and handmade silk flowers used in the arrangements. Yes, it's true; I glued every petal around a form to create roses and daisies. The food and the cake, all homemade, and my cousin's band would bring everything together for a beautiful celebration.

Even now as I write this, I am convicted that I spent no time on becoming closer to God so I could understand His plan for marriage. The strange part is that as the day came closer and closer, the crankier I got. Wasn't I doing the "right" thing? Who could I talk to? The invitations had already been sent, and the responses were coming back. People were traveling from Michigan, California, Ohio, and every part of New York. Whom could I tell that I was doubting all of this? I thought my sister was too young to understand. There were my new little sisters to be, but I couldn't tell them. How about my encouraging friends? I realized that I had rarely confided in them, that truly I had not confided in anyone about my doubts. It is apparent as I reflect on my feelings at that time, because I was a people pleaser, I had not wanted to disappoint anyone. My heart wasn't in this whole thing. I was just getting the project details done.

This is not a testament to bash anyone else for my decisions. It is an inspired writing from my heart that now belongs to God, the Father. It is always easier to look backward in life than to look forward to what we should do. God has taught me so much about learning how to seek His will. This is one of those times I wish that I could have known more of God's truth when I was younger.

Believe it or not, there was someone who figured out something wasn't right. Surprisingly, it was my younger brother Earl who recognized that I was not into this relationship as deeply as I should have been. He is still a very insightful, loving, and thoughtful younger brother. To this day, I remember him bringing someone I truly did love to our house for the rehearsal dinner. The moment I saw my brother's hunting buddy, I knew that I should not be marrying anyone at that time. This meeting took place on my parents' front porch while the rehearsal party was going on in the backyard. I actually considered running—racing away from everyone and not becoming anyone's wife. Running away was the reality. This marriage was giving me that opportunity to run away from my life. I loved my fiancé, Buddy, but I was learning more about him and it was not what I pictured as part of my life. He wasn't the person he appeared to be.

However, the dependable, driven, and desperate young woman that I was didn't take the way out God had again given to me. I am still grateful that my brother saw my heart. He will never know how loved I felt at that moment. I wish in that instant, the courage that I possessed would have been my strength. Instead, it was because of my pride, not my courage that I went through with this marriage, even with God providing me with ways of escape before we ever got to the church.

The morning of the wedding was one of the most miserable mornings I have ever experienced. My mom and I were at odds with each other about everything. It was obvious that she knew what I knew. This wedding was not the best thing for my future. She made it very clear that Buddy was not her choice for me. I wish she and I could have found a better way to communicate than to banter back and forth with hurtful jabs. How I wish that day could be a do over for my mom and me. She was trying to protect me, which I understood later when I became a mother. But at that moment, I just wanted someone to get me out of my perfectly detailed wedding.

The third and final opportunity to get out of this actually came as my dad was walking me down the aisle, those sweet, precious moments when a dad walks his little girl down the center of the church to hand her off to another man. My dad said to me, "Are you sure you want to do this?"

"Really...NOW! I'm the one in white, crying and confused."

Dad said, "We can turn around right now." I remember hesitating for a millisecond and wanting to do exactly that. Strike three! I kept going and I made it to the front where my fiancé and I both agreed to stay together forever. Once I got there and made that covenant promise, I believed that lifetime is how long this would last.

For many years, I thought those emotions were just pre-wedding "jitters." As I have grown in my relationship with God, He has shown me that He had given me several opportunities to escape that marriage. Consequently, learning to discern the will of God has become a quest in my spiritual growth. About six years almost to the day after that wedding, I completely surrendered my life to God, resulting in a personal relationship with Him through faith in Jesus Christ.

A lot of happiness and heartbreak occurred during those years between my marriage and my rebirth in Christ. Happiness included motherhood. I rejoiced in being the mom of two very amazing little girls at that time. They were now on this journey with God as well. Buddy had made an outward profession of a relationship with God, so at last we could truly dedicate our marriage to God. Hopefully, we could overcome the challenges of the first five years.

Unfortunately, there was no way for me to know where someone else was with God. If the outward is doing what seems to be the "right" thing, how can we know what is really in a person's heart? Just as I was so conflicted in my heart before the wedding and a few people had reached out to challenge me, God had brought some folks into our lives to challenge us to fulfill the vows of our marriage and work on what would draw us closer to God, which, in turn, would bring us closer together.

What I learned during the next few years is that prayer would be my greatest comfort. Studying God's word and fellowship with other believers became what I hungered for.

A revival meeting was being held at the little local church we had found to attend. I was drawn by God to pray for child number three to be a son who would have a heart for God, just like his dad. I was sure that would mean I would soon get pregnant and have a son. After all, God knew the heart of my husband. The warm loving environment of the bible belt geography had to be where God wanted us.

Well, I did get pregnant. Wow! My prayer was answered! However, all of a sudden, my husband no longer wanted to be in warm south. He sought to get a job working for a company in up north where his mother was employed, leaving me behind with two little girls, ages five and three and early pregnancy sickness. He fled to his mother. Morning sickness had lasted for at least the first four months each time I had gone through this before. Medication caused me to sleep. Not having an adult who was awake enough to care for these children was at best a disaster. God had not given me a desire or the strength to move back to his hometown. "Please, God, help us" was the cry of my heart. Being sick and weak and trying to take care of loud, energetic preschoolers were the words that described what my life involved, while I was also preparing to move back to his mother's house. The whole process was a blur. In August of that year, we finally were reunited as a family. We were expecting a baby in December, starting kindergarten with our five year old, and I was trying to build my faith and physical strength while caring for our three year old.

Finding a place to live in the capital area of his home state was brutal, but eventually in October we found a second story flat in a bigger city than I had ever lived. I was so thankful to God. Our landlord was a born again believer who attended a very lovely fundamental Bible believing church. As we settled in, we were struggling financially, emotionally, and spiritually. I wanted to be very involved while my husband seemed indifferent and no longer appeared to want anything to do with God.

December arrived and so did our third child. A girl? What? I had clearly prayed for a son with a heart for God like his father had. How could this be? Although I deeply loved and longed for God, I struggled to understand. Buddy was clearly disappointed with another girl. He was grumbling and obviously did not appreciate having to provide for all that our family needed. He expected me to leave two little ones in childcare while the older one was in school and go to work. The childcare would cost more than I could earn. This became several months of loneliness, heartache, and detachment. Within one year of arriving in the place he wanted to live, he no longer wanted our family, to be a husband, a father or a Christian was his declaration. He left to be with another woman. Our vows were destroyed; my faith was in need of critical care, and three little innocent children who had not asked for this were hurt.

This was the result of my not turning around on that wedding day. My three children were stuck with just me. I was now the only adult left to be responsible for providing for their physical, spiritual, and personal growth needs. I was committed to being a Godly parent to them. I truly had to rely on God's promise, "And my God will meet all our needs according to His glorious riches in Christ Jesus." Philippians 4:19

That was the moment of reality for needing God. We would not look to man to be our provider. Instead, we became a united family of faith. Heartache existed, but God was healing us. Humility was necessary. Being prideful would not be productive for our growth in Christ.

The lessons our family learned were long term. We realized that pleasing others was not healthy. But serving God by serving others was healthy. We found many ways to love and honor God by helping others. My daughters and I had to grow in our faith by studying His word together, ministering to others in all kinds of ways, praying, and praising God in all things. The broken pieces were finding their place in the mess that had been my life up to that point. God continued to teach us through His word, I Timothy 6:17, "Command those who are rich in this present world not to be arrogant nor to put their hope in wealth, which is so uncertain, but to put their hope in God, who richly provides us with everything for our enjoyment."

In spite of my not taking God's way out of that 1st marriage, God gave me the very precious gift of my daughters. They have grown up to be strong, determined, courageous, and loving servants of God, and for that, I am truly thankful.

Provision

IT IS LIKELY THAT MOST people put a jigsaw puzzle together the same way. Of course, we start by putting the border/corner pieces together first. Those pieces with a straight side or a perfect corner give a great clue to their position in the puzzle.

Maybe that is where I got the idea that if someone is smooth on one side, the crooked side will fit in somehow. This is not always the best way to be looking for the qualifications of a marriage partner. Nonetheless, that was the toolset that I had.

Knowing who someone is for a few years doesn't exactly mean you really know the person. It wasn't until many years and prayers after I married the first time that I realized this man was not fitting easily into my grand vision of life as a family.

It is not my desire to write about him, but rather what I learned as a result of my life experiences through those challenging years. He was someone I loved very much and grieved for a very long time when the pieces finally were scattered too far to try to gather them together.

Twelve years was the actual length of the marriage, but he was in and out like there was a revolving door. By the way, I hate revolving doors; I prefer the kind that you go in or out of—not getting stuck wondering where to go. He actually spent less than eight years actively participating. The best outcome of those years resulted in the three beautiful daughters God gave me.

He had made a similar profession of faith that July of 1988. One thing that I have come to know through walking through this lonely journey is that only God really knows the heart of anyone.

His final departure from our little family took place in October of 1990. Our youngest daughter was not even one year old, and the other girls were both less than two weeks away from birthdays that would make them five and seven years old. He simply told me that "This isn't who I am." In other words, being a husband, a father, and having a family wasn't who he was. Wait a minute. What about until death do us part and the vows before family and friends? All those memories and moments of the last eight years meant nothing. Who gets to quit in the middle of hardship? I was never one to give up. Somehow things would have to work out.

A few days later, it was revealed that not only was he gone, but he had left us for another woman who was raising a child on her own. He told me he felt bad for her. I believe he once referred to it as ministering to her. That was not a ministry I ever located anywhere in the scriptures. Then they became pregnant with a child together while he was still married to me.

My life was once again a ruined box of puzzle pieces ready to go to the attic and be left in the dark, lonely and unwanted.

It was during this time that I developed an unquenchable thirst for the word of God. Reading the Bible was my greatest comfort and learning from my pastor and Sunday school teachers how to study made it even more interesting. The Bible became alive, the living and breathing presence of God in my life. And I had Him to thank for the daughters He had given me.

My girls were my greatest joy on this earth, and they deserved a happy childhood. This was going to be difficult for me to provide with no money and bills and rent that had gone unpaid for months. I needed to find a new place to live and a new plan for how to provide a safe home and shelter for my family.

As a result of my brokenness and still having a child under the age of one who needed me, I had to resort to the humbling task of asking for help. The welfare system is certainly not a perfect solution for life's hardships, but for us at that time it was a temporary solution to giving me the chance to get my head cleared, regain the faith, strength, and courage I would need to face the days ahead. Walking into the social services office with my broken jigsaw puzzle of a life was one of the hardest days I have ever known.

These folks showed more kindness in the short time it took to get things in order than the friends and family who just wanted to express, "I told you so." They helped me allow the Lord to be our provider.

Having a place to live with food in the cupboards and time to laugh and play with my children is what life became. When days were hard, we would find a way to encourage someone else. Our pastor always told us if you start feeling like having a pity party, go be a blessing to someone else.

Lots can get accomplished when you decline the invitations to those lonely, depressing pity parties. My parents were concerned because they recognized that I was feeling so sad and lonely. They paid for me to take a cake decorating class. This kept me occupied for over a month. This developed into a hobby that allowed me to make and sell cakes. Consequently, I was too busy to attend the dark, not well attended sadness soirees. It is amazing how many people are encouraged when making or receiving a cake!

Who have you blessed recently? Don't let those pity party planners in. Keep them out and do something for someone else. Acts 20:35 is Paul teaching us this principle. "In everything I did, I showed you that by this kind of hard work we must help the weak, remembering the words the Lord Jesus himself said, 'It is more blessed to give that to receive.'"

Planting Flowers
before the Rain

HAVING SINGLE PARENTING THRUST ON me with no warning was not only life changing for me but also for my daughters, my parents, my friends, and my church family. These little girls were sweet, kind and caring children bringing my heart much comfort. So it became my mission and passion to make their childhood happy. I did not want my beautiful girls to have the pieces of their lives to be so scattered. We had enough of the drama and emotions with Daddy leaving. I did have a desire to have a son, but I was given three creative, intelligent, talented, and beautiful girls. The four of us learned to enjoy putting our jigsaw puzzle life back together, and we were determined that we were going to have fun while doing so.

Fun for us began with having to move to a different apartment. It had an open floor plan with a big kitchen and living room area, a small dining area, and two bedrooms. It was a recent renovation which had formerly been a grocery store. It was all new, providing us with a fresh, clean apartment to begin our new start.

Although we were strangers, the church we attended took us in immediately. Our new church family was a huge blessing to us whether it was helping us move or providing care for the girls. The people were amazing and taught me what true Christian love was. Their actions were a tremendous testimony to my family who lived over one hundred miles away. It was easily a one and a half hour drive one way to have any interaction with my family although my parents did all that they could to help as often as possible.

Of course, life wasn't without its continuing heartbreaks and disappointments. We worked through their heartache and tears when a promised visit from their father didn't happen. This occurred regularly and without any phone call to explain why. They were just three little girls excited to visit with this man, only to be disappointed because he would not communicate a reason for not showing up. The children had not asked for this, and I had purposed to always make the window of opportunity for them to spend time with their other parent a viable option. That way, down the road I could never be accused of keeping them apart. That continues to be my policy.

It was and still is my job to comfort them when they hurt or have disappointments. They are grown adult women with their own families now, and one of the things they love to do is tell stories from their childhood. They remember the fun things we did, the hard times we endured, and the many blessings of God during those times of transition to what our new family looked like—a mom and three lovely daughters. It reminded us of a television show, *The Brady Bunch*, a story about the fictional Brady family, except we didn't have Alice, the housekeeper, or Mr. Brady and his three sons! But we had our faith and our version of a 1990's modified family.

Helping with food and household supplies that we needed was the mission of our church family. When the girls' father and grandfather came and took our car away, the four of us were left alone in a city with no transportation. Unexpectantly, the church agreed to purchase a car for us. It was so amazing to feel such love from people we barely knew. It really taught us what real love was, the kind of love God has for us. Just as God's word says that we never have to worry about what we need because He will provide for us just as He does for the birds in the air (Matthew 6:26), God did provide for us through His generous servants.

Blessing those who had blessed us was important to us because there were so many who had done kind and loving things for us. The girls and I wanted to do something for all of them. As it turned out during that spring, someone had gotten dozens of flats of flowers which needed to be planted in the gardens around the church. We decided that if we could plant them, then they would bloom all summer as a reminder to all how thankful we were.

The dozens of flats represented hundreds and hundreds of plants to go into the soil that had been prepared. The weekend was the best time to accomplish our task. That Saturday the forecast was calling for rain, but we believed we could get it done early so that the Lord would have the rain water all the new transplants. Then on Sunday, the little flowers would welcome all the attendees. As a special treat, I had saved some of my housecleaning money from that week and had promised my daughters Chinese food as a blessing for all their hard work. The girls were still young but very willing to follow directions. With gloves and tiny shovels, we arrived by 8:00 a.m. to get to the task.

As we sorted the flowers and laid out the petunias, pansies, marigolds, and celosia, we were pleased with the design we had created. It took hours to dig tiny holes for each little plant, giving it its own space to grow and bloom. The girls were such diligent workers. As mid-morning approached, we realized that the rain was making its way toward us because we could see it coming from the western sky. This was a time to call out to God and ask Him to hear our prayers to just hold the rain until we could get all these baby plants into the ground. God did just that as we watched it get darker all around us, but the rain did not fall on our church grounds while we were on our knees planting and praying. The girls got more and more excited as they saw God answer their prayers. This experience was a huge boost both to our faith in the God of all creation and to our energy to finish the job. He was ministering to us as we were seeking to bless our newly found church family.

By the time we had cleaned up all the empty plant flats and packs and put our tools and gloves away, it was almost noon. As we got into our car given to us by the church, the rain started. We were amazed that the powerful God we loved had held the rain until we were safe inside our car. It was a moment we have never forgotten. It empowered our faith in the promise of God's word that He would provide and protect us as the Father to the fatherless. The rain poured and all the little plants were watered, and we didn't have to figure out a way to accomplish that. Chinese food had never tasted so good as it did that day, but every time we eat it, we are reminded about that amazing day we were serving Him.

Serving God always brings us joy regardless of whatever task we do that may be physically or emotionally demanding. Joy is the best component when seeking to make life fun. I truly believe that my daughters' childhood was blessed with joy in serving our Lord and Savior. That day for us helping others was the factor that made our lives so much fun. Fun doesn't always mean that children need to be entertained. Actually, it is more fun to teach children to bless others so that they can be filled with good childhood memories. My adult children know the satisfaction there is in serving Jesus, and that fills my heart with gratitude.

A fun childhood is one filled with love, adventures, and opportunities to serve others. To hear my children retelling this story with the awe and wonder of that day still sparkling in their eyes makes my mommy heart believe God truly was with us not only then but He continues to be.

Adopted for Christmas

UNTIL DECEMBER OF 1990 I believed that Christmas was the most wonderful time of the year. The words of that iconic Christmas melody express what most people feel about the holidays. It usually is a wonderful time of the year. However, unfortunately there are people who have a very difficult time at Christmas for many reasons.

For a child, Christmas should be filled with awe and wonder. This particular year, my heart ached for my little girls who were experiencing their own confusion and heartbreak. The word *wonderful* could not be used to describe that first holiday season without their dad. For all of us, the celebration was difficult, sad and lonely. What few traditions we had built in the eight-year life of our family were gone. It had always been Daddy who would cut down or buy a tree. It was also his job to get the lights all the way to the top of the tree. We would always visit both sets of grandparents and play games with family. But all that was changed forever. The girls had not even been visited by their dad with any regularity; consequently, they didn't get to see his side of their family at all. They missed their aunts and grandparents.

For us, that first Christmas as mom and daughters was filled with walking through stages of grief. We were experiencing shock, anger, denial, and depression. Their birthdays and Thanksgiving were the first family celebration casualties. The first year after a traumatic loss is filled with empty, broken, and shattered ideals. Not ever can that first trip around the calendar after heartache have many events called wonderful.

It was during the first twelve months when we became sensitive to the realization that other families were going through the same heartbreak of forever changed family holiday traditions. We saw the world through "blue" lenses. The popular Elvis song performed at Christmas about being blue at this joyous time would silence us when we heard it, and each of us would wipe tears from our eyes.

I had to be alert to the needs of my children and put away my own brokenness. My daughters would pray, asking God to have Santa bring their daddy back home. What a sight that would have been—a non-cooperative, defiant man wrapped in pretty paper with a bow on top of his head being dragged down the chimney by jolly St. Nick and left under our tree. At that point, I knew we needed some reality checks. Destroying this Christmas holiday was not my intention, but I discussed with them that only God can change someone's heart. I explained that Santa Claus is only a sweet story that parents chose to tell their children to make that time of year more mysterious and secretive.

I told my children that we had had enough lies and mystery, and I spoke a gentle loving truth to these precious little girls that Christmas. I shared that God was the really the only thing we had to celebrate. He was the gift-giver to all mankind. He had given us Jesus, the Savior of the world. As young ladies in training, they accepted the truth about the Christmas story, and their prayers no longer included the request for a special "daddy delivery" from jolly St. Nick. At the time, I did not realize the power of the Christmas truth I had shared with these early little evangelists!

The oldest daughter was in the first grade. She was so excited and bursting with joy for the love God had for her that she wanted everyone to know that same truth. So, she told her friends the WHOLE truth about Christmas. I didn't know that she had done this until I received a phone call from a mother who was hysterically screaming at me for ruining her Christmas. This woman whose family was intact with a loving husband and father and two healthy smart little boys living in a beautiful home was yelling at me, a single parent of three (ages seven and younger) who would be homeless after the first of the new year because the man of our family had chosen not to pay the rent for many months before his departure. We were looking for a new place to live with no money and only hope in God. How could I possibly have ruined her Christmas?

As I received her anger and bitterness, it occurred to me that her son was in my daughter's class at school. She finally finished ranting at me and hung up abruptly. I asked my oldest what had happened. She explained that she had told this young man how much God loved him. So, what was this woman so mad about? Her son thought that God's love for him was now his truth. This mother was enraged because her son no longer believed the "magic" of a chubby guy who wore a unique red outfit, trimmed in fur. This young boy had trusted in the love of God my daughter had shared with him. Truly, salvation is the best gift anyone can receive at Christmas.

I was not able to comfort this mother with that revelation. For all I know, she could still hate me. It had never been my intention to ruin her Christmas. My purpose was to help my children to realize that their dad could not somehow wind up in Santa's bag, be dragged through a chimney, and somehow magically appear under our tree. Santa represents an enjoyable and entertaining account for children, but the idea of "Santa" is not the solution to a family's reconciliation.

I determined that I needed to have a follow-up chat with my little ones about our truth not being everyone's way of celebrating. I explained that some mommies and daddies are okay with Santa being part of their Christmas traditions, and it is not for us to tell others whether they can use the Santa mystery. I clarified that we would just not let it be part of our Christmas joy because we were a unique family now. I knew that God was the father to these little girls now. Jesus taught us that HE is the way, the truth, and the life, and no one comes to the Father except through Him (John 14:6). Our family would rely on God's word and not believe that the folk stories told by men and women would be the answer to the trials in our lives. My children were not damaged by truth, and we never judged those who kept the myth of Santa alive.

Perhaps that first year was meant to be filled with a new understanding of truth and tradition. A wonderful family from our church blessed us with an invitation to their home for Sunday dinner and a walk in the fresh, crisp December air on the property God had given them. That walk was a precious reminder of God's magnificent creation. There were so many inspiring Christmas aromas—pine trees, lingering smoke from a wood fire, and the unspoiled scent of fresh cut lumber as we chopped down the perfect tree for our celebration. This new memory made with Godly people who wanted to bless us because they had been blessed by God was a perfect one to replace the broken ones playing in our minds.

The tree was shaped similar to me—short and stout! Much like the little teapot song we loved so much. The job of putting lights on the tree had never belonged to me before. This was a very difficult new responsibility, but I was getting used to the idea of facing new challenges head on. God would give me all the courage and strength that I would need; He was always with us.

Somewhere we have a great family photo of us under that pretty little tree. That first Christmas was the most difficult. However, we also learned a great deal about God's love through the generosity and kindness of others.

There were boxes of food and some thoughtful gifts from many of our church family. In the first weeks and months of the new journey we were forced to take, Miss Debbie and Miss Mary were our angels on earth. Those first milestones on our journey were celebrated with joy and love because of those two remarkable ladies and the amazing new church family. In those early times, Pastor and Mrs. B taught us so much about trusting God. The brief time from October through Christmas included all three of my daughters' birthdays, Thanksgiving, and Christmas. That was the roughest part of our journey; all of those "firsts" without Daddy were a part of us woven into the tapestry that God was creating. The Lord showed us His amazing love through the wonderful acts of His people, and we were forever changed.

The next six Christmas celebrations were much easier than that first one. We began to make new memories with fun, original traditions. As a result of little to no financial support, it was necessary to seek assistance during those solo parenting years. We were blessed to be adopted by many benevolent groups over the years.

One group that stands out in our memories if the freshmen class of a local pharmaceutical college during some time in the 1990's. It isn't the exact date that is critical to our remembrance but rather the actions of some determined young people who were spending their first year in a very difficult course of studies and labs. That was the "awe factor" for us. (Humorous side note: my youngest daughter got the opportunity to work at that college decades later. She saw firsthand how difficult their career path of education was.)

This class of eighteen and nineteen-year-old young people from all over the world were very generous to my ever-growing young family. They provided food, clothes, winter coats and boots, scarves, gloves, mittens, and, of course, some toys.

It still touches my heart more than a quarter century later, that some caring strangers took it upon themselves to abundantly bless us. I have often wondered if any of those future pharmacists have filled prescriptions for any of us since then. We know this for sure; that year, as a class they provided our physical and emotional needs that Christmas, filling our love tanks!

Typically, we don't think of hugging a pharmacist, but every year when the Christmas decorations come out, a piece of my heart sends hugs to that class of student pharmacists wherever they may be. God knows each of them, and we continue to ask Him to bless and save them.

We learned a lot about the kind and generous character of God during all kinds of circumstances and situations in those first years of being a family with just one parent. We learned that whether we have physical, emotional, or spiritual needs, God will find a way to fulfill them, sometimes using the kindness and generosity of people who are strangers to us.

It is critical to know and understand the reason we even celebrate

Christmas is because of our Savior. Our God came and showed us His abundant love for us. It was a love that was unselfish and self-sacrificing. This is the message I received from reading the Scriptures. Sharing what I have learned about the indescribable love of God is all I am asked to do in return.

"Then Jesus came to them and said, 'All authority in heaven and on earth has been given to me. Therefore, go and make disciples of all nations, baptizing them in the name of the Father and of the Son, and of the Holy Spirit, and teaching them to obey everything I have commanded you. And surely I am with you always, to the very end of the age." (Matthew 28:18-20)

Love came down and was laid in a manger so that one day He would be placed on a cross, and He would be brought back to life by the forgiving, merciful and gracious love of God. No greater love exists apart from the love of God. Because of this we can celebrate Christmas, commemorating the birth of Jesus, but more importantly we can celebrate life in Jesus!

Every Christmas may not be merry or bright. Lots of reasons can cause this situation. All it really means is that we need more of Christ. *Christ-more* is the true cry of the season. It is the love of God that makes things bright.

If you are going through that less than joyous season in your life, I challenge you to find someone to bless. Find a way to show more of Christ's love. God used all kinds of people to do that for us. The girls and I did not have to go through the first Christmas of being alone ever again. There is no doubt that was the hardest, but the amazing love of God has helped us heal from that heartache.

Our family has grown from our four to twenty in 2019. The memories of challenge and tears have faded, and we celebrate with great joy and thanksgiving just as we learned to do that first Christmas of change.

Our prayer is that regardless of whatever has challenged your world, you will turn everything over to God. Survive your circumstances by blessing others so that one day you will be able to smile at what situations God gave you the strength and courage to endure.

Wishing you a Christ-more season always!

Really? Ziti: An Answer to Prayer?

OFTEN PEOPLE HAVE ASKED ME, "What is the point of praying?" This is a question that I can jump all over with exciting and joyful answers. In my experience, I have learned that it is necessary to be prayerful in asking God to meet our needs. This became a profound part of my life as the job of parenting three little girls was left to be solely my responsibility. It was immediate that I realized that prayer was the greatest source of provision for our needs—all of our needs.

The physical necessities of food, shelter, and transportation were met by God who heard our prayers. Needing a place to live, we asked God to help us. Not only did He provide an apartment that didn't remind us of the departure of Daddy but one that was fresh and newly remodeled. God answered prayers for a car that safely would take the girls to school each day. We lived in a school district with no bus transportation. This left my young daughters having to walk to school in the worst weather while I strolled their baby sister alone through those unpleasant days (to and from school). God heard our cries for a way to get them to school and to medical appointments.

He stirred the hearts of people in our church to provide a car for us. A white Dodge Omni was God's answer.

There is a funny story that happened with that car when the pastor needed to use it one day. Because of a recurring physical trauma, I was laid up in back pain. For whatever reason, my back had flared up in extreme pain with muscle spasms that landed me on bed rest for about four to six weeks. This occurred early in my single parenting time. Our pastor was the most encouraging counselor of God's word I had ever met, and I was thrilled to be able to give him use of God's little Dodge Omni that the church had given us. Only a few hours later, he called me to tell me the engine had blown. We were both thankful that the girls and I hadn't been the ones to be stranded. Once again the Lord was meeting our needs with the help of our precious church family.

It occurred to me that many people could sing that old "Hee Haw" song about "gloom, despair, and agony on me . . . if it weren't for bad luck, I'd have no luck at all," but that is not at all how the girls and I saw it. We were thankful, always finding God's thread of silver and gold sparking in the darkness that tried to engulf us. Psalm 68:5 became our battle cry, "A father to the fatherless, a defender of widows, is God in His holy dwelling."

With no earthly father to help, provide, or protect us, we realized that God would do all of these things, and He was doing just that. He had placed our lonely little tribe in a wonderful church family. He was hearing our prayers and answering them abundantly. All that God was doing was showing us that our faith was what was growing. We rejected bitterness and sought to be a forgiving, prayerful family under God's authority.

This led to a new practice in our lives to have what we called

"Family Altar Time." This was a special time when we would gather around our coffee table in the living room and connect with each other and most importantly with God. This would happen briefly throughout the days of the week, but it was regularly enjoyed by all of us on Saturdays. The Saturday altar times were extra special because we could do it in the afternoon and not be rushed by bedtime or chores that were both necessary to keep us in order. We would talk about our week, what our blessings had been, and what our concerns were. This was often a time of putting our reliance on God even deeper, always seeking to include God in our daily lives.

The blessings listed almost always included being thankful that the girls had so many friends who came and stayed overnight on Fridays and Saturdays. They have always had the gift of hospitality, and nearly thirty years later, they still include this important part of living out their faith. They would always count our church family as huge blessings, especially Pastor and Mrs. B were lifted up in the girls' prayers, asking for them to have a special blessing from God. Praying for all of the people who poured into our lives regularly was so energizing.

Along with blessings, it was always necessary to talk about our concerns. Every one of us always listed Daddy as our biggest concern. We prayed fervently for him to "repent to the acknowledging of the truth." We prayed for his heart to be turned over to God. We don't know if those prayers ever have been answered; that is between him and God. But we know we tried in every way to show him God's love and the power of His forgiveness.

It was one particular Saturday altar time that sticks out in my mind as a profound reminder to be obedient to pray as well as the blessing of obeying the prompting of the Holy Spirit. The end of the month was always a more challenging time when it came to making the groceries last. One of the most important things I had learned was that planning and preparation made it easier for one adult to get three little girls ready for anything. Saturdays were great days to plan for the week and to prepare for those plans.

On that extra special Saturday, we were deciding what food we could make in the last days of this month. The girls longed to have baked ziti the next day. Well, this would be impossible to do with what I had in the cupboards or in my wallet. They said to me, "Let's pray for God to give us baked ziti!" How could I say no to that? Somehow God would best be the one to go to when something is impossible to do. This was a teachable opportunity for all of us. Would praying specifically really be that important to our amazing God? We would only have to wait until the next day to find out how He would answer.

As we finished altar time with singing, I stored up each moment in my mind as precious treasure. Worship with these rapidly growing Godly little children. Worship was so pure and holy, their voices singing to the Lord is still one of the sweetest sounds I have ever heard.

We continued with our typical Saturday tasks—laundry, laundry, and oh, yes, more laundry. Washing, drying, and folding repeatedly. Typically, about four loads would do it—darks, lights, whites, and towels. Actually, I love to do laundry, which is not what you hear most women say. The girls learned to be helpful with laundry and other household chores at a very early age. We always tried to make it fun and enjoyable to work together. Dusting, vacuuming, and tidying our house was gratifying.

As we finished our productive Saturday, it was part of our

routine to lay out the clothes for church and to set the table for breakfast the next morning. This made Sunday morning much less rushed and easier to get us all ready simultaneously so we could be at church and on time for our Sunday school classes. Of course, one could never plan for some disruptions like bloody noses or stockings that ripped, but we managed. It was normal for us all to be in our Sunday clothes, Bibles in hand, and hearts ready as we arrived five-ten minutes early each week.

That Sunday began as normal as any other, but the difference came at the end of the service. After I had gathered up my little lambs, I noticed another young mother beckoning me to speak with her. She and her husband currently had three children under the age of four and she was expecting again. She was so full of grace and love as she asked me, "Would you be offended if I gave your family something for your dinner?" Of course, being humbled to receive the blessing from others was a life lesson we had learned early on. I assured her we would be grateful and that it was very sweet of her to think of us. She quickly told me the story of her Saturday. As she was preparing for her Sunday to go smoothly, she felt the Holy Spirit leading her to make an extra dish of the meal she was getting ready for her family. She obeyed the prompting of God to make the meal but hadn't had a chance to call and let me know. We laughed as she told the story and exchanged our love and gratitude toward each other.

So, I asked, "What did you make?" You guessed it . . . Baked Ziti! I began to cry, and I asked her when she was preparing the meal. As we chatted back and forth, it was very apparent that just as these little girls were humbly bowed in prayer graciously asking the

Holy God of the universe for baked ziti, He was hearing them and inspiring this very busy young mother to make the blessing happen.

That Sunday meal was provided by God, just as He always provided but that meal was filled with an extraordinary boost of faith. When we pray, God hears us; He leads others to help meet our needs. This pan of baked ziti was a symphony of God's amazing omnipotence.

He is all powerful to give us the ability and desire to humble our hearts before Him and pray. It is equally in His amazing omniscience to lay on our hearts actions that can meet the needs of others.

Baked ziti is a family favorite for many more reasons that just tasting good. It is a reminder of tasting and seeing how good and faithful God is. Thank you, Lord, for your communication with us through prayer.

Messy Meatballs

IN THE YEARS OF SOLO parenting, it was apparent to me that it was totally my responsibility to manage everything from all the bills to baby dolls; baby dolls were the easy part. Groceries, rent, and heat were always the difficult part. Nevertheless, one thing in our faith that always energized us was being good stewards of hospitality. We loved enjoying meals and fellowship with all kinds of folks.

It was typical to plan meals ahead and invite some friends for either Saturday night or Sunday afternoon. That always involved organizing the food wisely. With the assistance we received, it required a lot of prayer and creativity to make the food last. For instance, homemade spaghetti sauce and meatballs was a meal we could make ahead, share with others, and still enjoy leftovers.

My daughters learned early in life to be great helpers. Even long before our family life was turned upside down, they were helping in the kitchen. Household chores, appropriate for their age, are vital to teach to toddlers. Children embrace being part of the community of their home, and they glow when they realize how helpful they are. The girls also were amazing baking assistants, helping to make, bake, and decorate cakes. If you have never decorated cakes, you would not imagine the dirty dishes that process creates. These very helpful young ladies were supporting our family by assisting in cleaning those messes frequently. To this day, these now grown women are wonderful cooks and very organized and tidy housekeepers.

Ministry is serving others in whatever capacity that we can so welcoming people into our home was the calling we had. This taught us all to have servants' hearts and share what very little we had. Although it wasn't much, it belonged to the Lord. As we shared with others, the Lord blessed us by multiplying our encouragement.

Once the girls were older in their early teens and I was working full time, they took on more responsibility in our home. Cooking meatballs together was the way we always did it, and I thought on this particular occasion that they were ready to do it on their own. I may have misjudged the explanation of my instructions.

In order to maximize our grocery dollars, I could often get a better value when buying in bulk. Ground beef was best to be bought in the large family packs. A budget pack of meat could often have over five pounds that would be split to provide for several meals. Meatballs would require about a pound and a half from the large package. For young women learning all the skills they needed to manage their own homes one day, this was a master test. Being able to use fractions is a vital part of home meal preparations. Maybe that's why cooking at home has become a lost art. Almost everyone hates fractions! I don't know if the girls hated fractions or if they just didn't understand them. Clearly, I didn't explain them well enough because the story I am about to tell you will demonstrate my responsibility in this. The girls are innocent of any error in the process of making the meatballs.

The sauce was the easy part. They just had to dump the cans of tomatoes, crushed and whole, and the spices which I had measured out the night before and placed into a baggie. No problem. The sauce was complete.

Meatballs. I "knew" the girls were ready, and they were—but my being home would have been a better scenario. So, they had mixed the meatball ingredients, and they were happy to roll all those meatballs. It was when I arrived home from work that we found that there was an issue.

I was so excited to see what they had created. They were growing up so fast. Already thirteen, eleven, and six years old, they were very skilled in their homemaking abilities. The apartment smelled like an amazing Italian restaurant. The oregano and basil were such pleasant aromas when swimming in the tomatoes. When I got to the stove, it was my plan to pull out one of their perfectly round balls of flavor and devour it. Instead of a pot filled with little round meatballs, I discovered a pot of tomato sauce with a near solid mass of meat!

It was one of those times that could either build up or tear down. As I look back, I'm sure I did not take the high road initially. Most probably we could call it the road of flesh response until I reached a crossroads of choosing a spirit-filled road or extended travel on the flesh road of disappointment and discouragement. At that crossroads, it was necessary not to make a mountain out of meatballs. Living for some years alone with no husband had taught me to be flexible. Our plans would have to take a re-route. This situation required one of those re-directed paths.

The girls had used the entire value pack of ground beef rather than one-third. This may have been okay if they had not stirred them right away. The meat needed time to cook into its shape, but the girls saw the pot getting too full and were concerned about the top ones not getting cooked. The logic of why they stirred the pot was correct; it was the amount of meat that made the situation messy.

Messy meatballs are not the worst thing that can happen in one's life. We figured out a way to remove the meat mass into pans and bake them as Italian meatloaves. The girls were devastated that they had made a mistake. It was important to remind them about how helpful they had been and that one day this wouldn't matter. This was one of those moments to learn from what happened and to move forward.

What possibly can be learned from this? Well, actually a very essential lesson: We <u>are</u> going to make messes while we learn. The important thing is to learn from our mess and move forward with the new information we have learned.

It is imperative to also impart a lesson from God's word in our messy meatball misery! God is forgiving. He forgives us, and it is not brought up again to hurt us. Our memories should remind us about the lessons we have learned. All the things for which God has forgiven us are gone and in the past. This story is not written or brought up to humiliate anyone. We remember with a sense of humor and lasting memory to show mercy to others as they make "messes." Just as my daughters have grown to become amazing cooks because they were given the opportunity to learn from their failures and to try again. With each new attempt life becomes less messy.

We can equate this principle to our relationship with God. He understands that we are going to get "messy" as we will make mistakes, especially when we try to do something without Him. The beauty of His mercy is that He allows us to get up and try again. However, as we continue to accomplish things, we need to include God's leading and strength, even in making meatballs!

Trip to New Jersey

AMONG THE MANY VALUES TAUGHT throughout the Scriptures, friendship is one with which I have had many life-giving experiences. Over the course of my life, I have had the privilege of developing close friendships with many Christ-loving families, couples, and singles whose inspiration has shaped my girls and me in significant ways. Our lives were intertwined so intimately that we were able to share truth and encouragement with one another in our deepest sorrows and highest joys.

One remarkable young lady walked through her courtship during the season of our close friendship. It was a joy and a privilege to watch her and her special young man navigate various challenges and take their relationship to the throne of Jesus, leading to a wedding and a marriage that glorified God in every way. My daughters were asked to be in a youth choir that sang in their wedding. Although the girls were very excited, they were also blessed to be a part of such a great celebration. The young couple moved to New Jersey shortly after the wedding. We loved and missed them very much.

In 1997, this exceptional young couple played a significant role in our lives. The doctors had been trying to find the cause for several medical problems I was experiencing. The news of a tumor on my pituitary gland that needed to be removed was overwhelming. Almost seven full years as a single mom enduring lots of challenges and hurdles, and yet this one slammed me in every way. It was the end of the school year in late June. The girls needed to celebrate the end of a successful school year, and I needed spiritual wisdom. When I called my friends in New Jersey, I told them we missed them and explained we had some concerns. I asked if we could spend time with them to seek their prayer support and wisdom.

After completing our plans, we embarked on our adventure to New Jersey. We felt so welcome in their home. As we observed the love they had for God and for each other, our hearts, minds, and bodies were able to rest and be revived. What peace there was in doing devotions with this couple!

While we were visiting with them, these friends wanted to provide something special for the girls, so they blessed us with tickets to spend a day at a large amusement park. Since my dear friend was going with us, I knew the girls would have fun because I did not and would not ride on a rollercoaster. My head was spinning with all the "what if's" of upcoming surgery and how that would impact our family; therefore, a rollercoaster or ride of any kind was not on my agenda. Our desire was for the girls to have a fun day with special memories, and I must say that day at the park indeed provided memories that we all hold dear to this day.

Ironically, I began to think that the girls needed to see me attempt these enormously terrifying rides. So that is what they saw! First was the rollercoaster ride. I was terrified until we came to the top, and as we began the plunge, I found some relief and enjoyment. With the emboldened power of surviving a rollercoaster, I got on the next one, a rotating twist-a-whirl, tilt-a-whirl, or something like that. DONE, I was done! I suggested Emi take the girls for a bit. I was so dizzy that I found the first bench that I could, and I PARKED myself. Everything but the bench was spinning. Questions were circling in my head:

"What have I done?"

"How can I get us home?"

"How will the girls survive without me?"

"Who will raise the girls?"

"God, what have I done? Please show me our future."

"Please give me peace."

It was as if I were in a cloud where all I could see was all the doubt and fears just being spun in my head. I must say, this surely is not the way I would ever suggest to others to shake up their minds. While I was in this foggy state, Emi and the girls walked by me three times, without my noticing. The fourth time they stopped and asked if I were okay! After a lovely cold drink and a few more minutes of non-motion, I was able to enjoy the rest of the day with them. The cloud in my head lifted and the sun shone all around us!

Prayer for God's direction, His wisdom and healing were the jewels of the quest we had sought and desired. God answered through this young couple who gave me the wise counsel to believe that God was enough. I felt such deep contentment, even in my circumstances, and I knew I was so blessed to have friends like these. As they poured out their love to us, we rejoiced in who God was and what He was going to do when we got home.

The ride home was filled with peace and contentment because I recognized in a way that I had never really understood before that our future was in God's hands. I was prepared to walk through the days ahead. I was reminded of Psalm 16:8-9 which says, "I have set the Lord always before me. Because He is my right hand, I will not be shaken. Therefore, my heart is glad and my tongue rejoices. My body will also rest secure." How amazing is the living word of God!

> [Side note: A "funny" thing occurred as I was writing this story. I was listening to an old Scripture Memory Album. The song about not being shaken came on as I wrote about the dizzy spell! I love God's sense of humor. How can I not have joy when He uses so many avenues to remind me of the truth in His WORD? Indeed, I will not be shaken.]

Our lives were changed in powerful ways during that weekend. When we returned home, the answering machine was filled with messages. This was long before cell phones were carried by everyone. One of those messages was to cancel the doctor's appointment that had been set to discuss and schedule my surgery. The message relayed that there had been a mistake in reading the CT scan and that there was no tumor at all.

WHAT?? Had God shaken the tumor right off the pictures that had been taken? I couldn't believe this so I called them the next day, and they confirmed that there really had been a mistake in reading the results and there was no tumor. This was such astounding news! I was not going to have to struggle anymore with questioning who would raise my kids. God had protected me and delivered me to a place of peace that passes all understanding.

We arrived home from our trip on the 1st of July 1997. We planned to enjoy a few days of vacation at home together and then celebrate the 4th of July with our church. The other messages on the answering machine were interesting but did not seem to be life changing like the one from the doctor's office. My friend Sally from a local singles introduction business had given my information to some of the gentlemen who fit the matching criteria. Of course, some called while I was gone. One man had five children that he was raising alone. WOW—a total of eight children before we even had a conversation! I actually decided to give this guy a call. We had a simple introductory chat, and he definitely seemed to have potential, but there was an abrupt end to our dialog as someone's child had an urgent need.

Another gentleman had left three messages. Each message seemed sadder and lonelier sounding that the previous one. I felt that I needed to get back to him and let him know we had been away for the weekend. When I called him, his voice sounded gentle and kind. I reassured him that I was not trying to be rude by not returning his calls, but the girls and I had been away, enjoying a peace-filled weekend with close friends. As we talked, our conversation seemed to be filled with curiosity and wonder. Then I asked him where he went to church. That was it; there had to be something that wouldn't work out. I was now content in being a single mom, and this man didn't attend any church. So he surely would not make any of my lists! I learned that he was formerly involved with a very well known cult. I told him I had enjoyed talking with him, but that we would not be able to pursue any kind of relationship because the teaching he had was from a cult of false teaching.

The really neat thing is that at my church we had just completed a several month study on false teachers and how to share the truth of the gospel with them. Maybe, this was an opportunity to speak truth. Our pastor had taught how difficult it is to witness to followers of false teaching. They are told not to even hear what someone else tells them. Therefore, it can be impossible to speak truth into their hearts because they won't listen. However, I took God literally when I read from His word that nothing is impossible for God (Luke 1:37). I realized that even leading a person who trusted in the teachings of the false religion could be redeemed by God.

I told this charming gentleman that it would not be possible to pursue a relationship because of his religion. I explained that I was only interested in someone who would pursue a personal relationship with God the father, the Son, and the Holy Spirit. I thought this would be the end of our connection. Yet, he said these golden words, "But, wait. I have questions! That is the reason I stopped attending. I had questions that they did't want me to ask." I will never forget that statement. He opened the door; he was seeking and asking for answers! God was giving me an opportunity to share the truth for the questions he had. It was such a spiritual blessing to hear the heart of this man as he realized the doubts of his faith had finally been answered. He had been brought up in a religion founded by a convicted con man nineteen hundred years after the work of God's Son on the cross. The "bible" from this group was not translated from any of the Greek or Hebrew scholars. Their version falsely changed some scripture to adapt to their beliefs that denied the deity of Jesus.

This beautiful man was hungering and thirsting for God's word. We talked about salvation, and he understood that spiritually he could not do enough good works to earn eternal life. It was so incredible to share the truths of God with someone who deeply wanted answers. This man's name is Rondelle.

Rondelle met me and my girls the next day (July 2), and on Friday, July 4, he came with us to our church celebration. He met everyone I held dear in my faith family. We spent the day with his son and we had a blast all together. A few days later, he sat with my pastor. The following weekend, I introduced him to my parents and extended family. On July 19, 1997, Rondelle and I were married in his home in the presence of friends and family. Yes, that is after only seventeen days of knowing each other. Yes, that is UNHEARD OF. We do not recommend this to anyone whose heart is not totally surrendered to Jesus. Our journey began with faith and it endures because of our continued trust in God who has blessed us with love, commitment and confidence.

I began that adventure in June 1997 with a desperate, scared, and broken heart. However, through fellowship with gentle, loving friends, my heart found peace and contentment. That rejuvenation in my soul led me to the greatest opportunity of being used by God to share the deepest truth in my life with Rondelle. We now shared a mutual faith that led us to humble ourselves before God and allow Him to guide us into what He wanted us to be—a couple that could raise a blended family through the challenges and trials of life while still bringing honor and glory to Him, and parents who could conceive a child in the love which is meant to be between the parents of a child.

Our story is not finished yet, but the journey together has filled the pages of our lives for over twenty-three years. Our family brings us so much joy. They are all adults; four of our five are married and have children, giving us the privilege of being called "Papa" and "Grammy." What a wonderful blessing this journey next to Rondelle has been. We pray we will always be able to share God's goodness to us in stories and testimonies of laughter and tears. May you be encouraged to know the same God who created the heavens and the earth loves you, and He desires a personal relationship with each and every one of us.

Special Anniversary

ANNIVERSARIES ARE A TIME TO stop, reflect, and remember. It can be the anniversary of the death of a loved one whom you deeply miss or of a decision that changed the course of life many years ago or, of course, the anniversary of a couple's marriage. On the other hand, anniversaries can be a time to celebrate, reminisce, be thankful, and look to the future. This particular year was a nothing special wedding anniversary for us (my 2nd husband, Rondelle)— seventeen years of walking through life together. We've enjoyed the birth of a child, the graduations and marriages of our children, and also the heartaches of losing parents and loved ones. Why should seventeen be anything special? Because that is the number our son Anthony wears on his baseball uniform. (And by the way, he had an amazing baseball season that summer.)

Why does "seventeen" mean anything? Well, seventeen years ago, a fine man was introduced to a lonely single mother of three little girls. It was just before I had plans to leave for an end-of-school year get away weekend that I got a call from (my friend) Sally. She wanted to introduce me to a couple of possible romantic connections for me since she worked for an introduction service. They screened people and matched them according to faith, personality, etc. No pictures were allowed, so that any matches would not be based on physical attraction. I told Sally this was to be the last time she attempted to set me up because I believed I needed to be content raising my three young daughters, who were now seven, eleven, and thirteen years old. I explained that we really were doing well, and although it would be nice to share my life with a real man, he would have to love the four of us as a package deal. I believed it would take a miracle from God. It was amazing how thoughtless men could be when they would meet me, first showing interest and then upon learning that I had children, saying, "You have three kids!" as if it was a revelation to me.

Sally was determined she could find the "right" guy who would not be overwhelmed that I was raising a family by myself. So she gave my number to the last two gentlemen that she had.

The girls and I had gone to New Jersey and enjoyed a lovely weekend with friends, having the opportunity to visit Hersey, PA, and experience a marvelous time at Six Flags, NJ. All the way home, we sang and praised God, and I realized that I truly was content just to be with my daughters.

The answering machine was full when we arrived home on July 1, 1997. There were messages from both of the guys Sally wanted me to meet. I prayed before calling either back. It was so nice to just talk and not be pressured to wonder if I were going to be found attractive by either one. Gentleman #1, I'm sorry I don't remember his name, had a great voice; he loved God and he was raising five kids by himself. I caught myself almost saying out loud, "You have five kids!" as if it would be a revelation to him. We chatted briefly, and with various children needing something, we agreed to chat again sometime.

The second gentleman, Rondelle, had called three times, leaving a message each time and sounding sadder than the time before. He apparently hadn't considered that I could be out of town. He just thought I wasn't calling him back. His last message was so sad that I had to call and let him know we had been away. Talking to Rondelle was as natural and effortless as breathing. He asked me great questions, and I found out that he had been raised as a Jehovah's Witness. The red flags were up and flying, so I thanked him for a lovely chat, realizing that our faith systems of belief were very different. Having just finished a six week study in false teachings, I was confident that we could not agree on major doctrines. I was confident in telling him we did not share the same beliefs. He then said the most amazing thing. He replied, "I have questions about my own faith." That was the opening of a door to share all of the truths I had just spent several weeks studying. I was blessed to share the history of his faith which is not something his "church" wants their followers to know. He was hungry with questions about what he believed. The teachings he had received had caused so many doubts that he wasn't sure what to believe.

This man was willing to meet with my pastor the very next weekend! The church the girls and I attended was hosting a July 4th party, and Rondelle was delighted to come. However, the very next day, July 2nd, he wanted to meet my family. We agreed that it would happen that night.

The girls were protective of me. They knew that for seven years I had hoped and prayed that their dad would come back and that had not happened. They were determined that no one would hurt me again. The moment the knock came at the door, my daughters were there before I could get up. Rondelle brought Doritos and other snacks for them. His act of thoughtfulness to consider the kids first was beyond my ability to understand that it was God who brought this man to meet us.

The most unbelievable piece of this puzzle is that seventeen days later, we were married. This time it wasn't about the ceremony or details of flowers and such. This relationship had barely begun but we were committed to a relationship with GOD and he met with my Pastor and also with my parents. He knew that I had three girls that needed a Dad and he is that and more to my children and grandchildren. He was raising a son on his own, who became my sweet son and then we were blessed with the birth of a little boy. He was the answer to that prayer of so many years earlier when I prayed to have the son of a godly man. Rondelle is that man and the love in his eyes at the birth of our son filled my heart to overflowing. I had given birth before and never knew that kind of heavenly love. There is of course a lot more to this story that involves prayer and cancer and laughter and tears, but although that 17th anniversary was years ago now I am still blessed to celebrate any years of my life with this man.

Mom's Death

CANCER IS A WORD THAT brings darkness to the brightest and most beautiful of any life. For many years, the word *cancer* has meant death. The treatment for cancer was more like torment. I watched my parents grieve their loved ones who were struck with the various types of cancer. Was it environmental, predisposition, or just part of the path they had to walk on this earth? I observed grief at its most organic state when watching Mom and Dad bury folks who were so dear to them.

My father was one of sixteen children so there were many aunts, uncles, and cousins. The second born was my dad's older brother Howard. Dad often told us to pack the car because we were "going for a ride." It came to be more often than not that "going for a ride" was another way of saying we were going to visit Uncle Howard and his sweet tiny wife, Aunt Thelma. He and Dad would walk around the property and talk about the gardening and landscaping plans. Aunt Thelma would find a game to play with us or a craft to do! She is my forever inspiration anytime I do a cross-stitch project. Their two sons were grown—much older than the three younger children of the six that Mom and Dad toted around.

Those memories became very precious to me as Dad began to visit Uncle Howard in the hospital, only he went alone. The love of a brother gave my dad the strength to watch Uncle Howard succumb to hideous brain cancer. As a young high school student, I was about the same age as Uncle Howard's grandchildren when he passed away. Observing someone's grief is raw and heartbreaking, especially when that someone is your father. Dad sobbed and cried with desperation of being separated from a brother he loved so much. My older brothers, uncles, and cousins had to pry my father from the casket. It was the intense pain of grief my father had tucked away to be strong for our family when my brother had died more than ten years earlier. The compressed, repressed, and unexpressed grief of the love my father had for his son and brother had found a way to escape.

Seeing my dad be so real, so broken made me love him even more, knowing he sacrificed his own pain to try to comfort my mom and brothers all those years. He was the strongest man I had ever known.

Well, of course, the years continued to pass by and the pages of the calendar of life were gone before we realized it. It was my mother who would be diagnosed with that deplorable word-*cancer*. It was small cell lung cancer, very aggressive and not treatable. She would not have long to live.

My mind went back to my father going through the process with Uncle Howard. I asked myself, could Dad do this? Would he have the strength to do this?

The diagnosis came in mid-July. By September each day was an amazing gift. Mom insisted on trying chemotherapy although most of her caregivers and doctors did not recommend it. Their concern was that it would destroy what quality of life she had left. Only one doctor was willing to experiment on her, and she was ready to fight. The only treatment she received was on Friday, September 7, 2001. Four days later, September 11th I packed the truck so that my youngest child and I could visit Grandma. I put praise music on—no TV or radio news; it was time to praise God and pray for His grace to pour down on our family.

When we arrived at Grandma and Papa's, we found a battlefield of chaos. My mom was vomiting and unable to control her bodily functions. On top of this awful scenario, it looked as if her skin had been dipped in acid. It was the most violent reaction to one treatment of chemotherapy that any of the medical experts had ever seen. We observed her saying bizarre things and being almost hallucinogenic. The ambulance couldn't get there fast enough. While we were trying to care for Mom, my sweet baby sister arrived and was in a horrified state. I wondered, "How does she know about Mom?" Dad and I had not had a chance to call anyone. It turned out she was so upset because of what was happening in the world—September 11, 2001, New York City and Washington, D.C., had been attacked. I was so glad my mom was unaware of any of this news. She would have been unable to stop crying for all the losses that day because she was a woman with strong feelings of empathy.

Once she was stabilized at the hospital, it was determined that she was experiencing excessive mini-strokes which were damaging her brain. The cancer was continuing to aggressively multiply. No more chemotherapy would be done; her quality of life had been destroyed.

Decisions about where she would spend her final days had to be made. At my last visit with her, she had been able to verbalize to me that she did not want to die with strangers. She wanted to

IMA C. TOOITT

die at home with her comfortable scenes and precious memories surrounding her. This is where I once again saw my dad be the strongest love of my mom's life. He made the decision that she would come home, and I would live with them to care for Mom. Joining us was my three-year- old son and sixth grade daughter who had just started home schooling. Middle school was brutal, and Grandma's battle was enough for her little heart to deal with.

We moved down on a Sunday, and Mom was scheduled to be brought home via ambulance on Tuesday. Preparations for a hospital bed and hospice care were already made. She had a very bad night on Monday, so they postponed homecoming to Wednesday. That was the day she returned to the dwelling she had shared with my dad. She was weak and unable to clearly communicate, but her eyes told the story that she knew she was home. Hospice care and family visiting is what completed that day. Thursday was a new day. More visits and instruction came from the hospice nurses. What a tremendous service they provide to the entire family of a seriously ill loved one!

My sister and I observed Mom's hands trying to move. It was as if she was trying to stir something. We giggled as we both realized that in her mind she was cooking for us! She had spent her life caring for all of us so this was only natural for her. We gently reassured her that she had done a great job and she could rest now because her chores were finished. She became still and rested.

A bit of time passed and her hands began to move again, only this time it appeared that she was knitting. She frequently was making something and there was an afghan that she had not finished. Again, my sister and I giggled—she was "finishing" the knitting project! We both assured her that she had done a beautiful job and all she had to do was rest.

As my dad spent the day sitting with her, he would draw close and she would be concerned and try to utter the words "careful" and "babies." It seemed as if she had babies in bed with her, which didn't really surprise us. The greatest joy that my mother had ever known was being a mom. She had previously sent a fourteen-year-old son and several miscarried babies ahead to Jesus's care.

That Thursday night everyone was so tired we went into peaceful sleep. In the early morning hours, I was awakened by a spirit, an unknown presence. I very quickly but quietly went to check on Mom. She was still alive, but her breathing had changed. It was no longer so labored; it was shallow, but peaceful. She was very near the end, and the spiritual presence clearly was not allowing her to be alone as she left her earthly life, entering into the kingdom of her Savior Jesus Christ.

My dad was holding her hand as she breathed her last breath. It was a peaceful, beautiful moment. His strength and love for her was evidenced by the tears he could not stop as they rolled down his face.

Being present for my mother's passing was one of the most spiritual moments in my life as a believer in the promises written in the Word of God. Jesus was the way, the truth, and the life for me in that moment as well as for so many others. Mom and Dad's pastor came and did a brief, beautiful service for our intimate family before taking her body away it was the loveliest way to prepare us for the weariness of the next few days.

It was then that I understood the grief that my dad had at Uncle Howard's funeral. Telling someone goodbye is never easy, but it is a part of life. Having the power of God in times of grief or joy is the greatest benefit of belonging and surrendering our lives to the Lord Jesus on this side of the grave. I believe that Jesus will bring us all together again one day. That is the hope He has promised! "For now we see only a reflection as in a mirror, then we shall see face to face. Now I know in part; then I shall know fully, even as I am fully known (I Corinthians 13:12).

Detention

TRAVELING IS A SECRET PASSION of mine. I love packing kids and kinfolk and heading off for an adventure; many of these adventures have taken me to lots of places. The beaches of South Carolina are some of our favorite destinations. As my children have grown and left the nest, the adventures also have changed.

One particular spring break is etched in the chronicles of my mind forever. This trip was just about my two sons and me. The three of us were driving to Michigan to visit family.

I had always enjoyed the special trips that I got to take with my daughters. Girls and their moms should have those opportunities, which create sweet memories to be treasured beyond the span of generations. What a gift this was to be able travel with my sons as well.

Getting ready for this big memory making excursion required planning, packing, and preparing for a fun week with my boys. The oldest son was a senior in high school and TJ, the baby of the family, was in Kindergarten. These two young men that God had entrusted to my husband and me to raise were in the midst of very important years in their lives, one completing the states required education standards and one at the beginning. We continually prayed for wisdom to give these young men the desire to serve God and do well all the time. As it turned out, this trip actually would provide me an opportunity to teach my sons by example.

In all of the excitement for a mom and her sons embarking on their adventure, it never occurred to me that our directions had routed us on a brief shortcut through Canada rather than going through Ohio, the longer distance. Lovely people who are very kind and have interesting ways of pronouncing a language we share live in Canada, our neighbor to the North. It was post 2001 so terrorist security was in its full glory, especially at the airports, but traveling by car shouldn't be a concern or so we thought.

Being honest was a principle that I was taught as I was growing up. However, I had been caught in a lie concerning a young man's work- book. It happened when I was in first grade. The boy was a "pain," always pulling my pigtails! His smile was so cute though. Hiding his workbook seemed like a fun little trick to play on this impish classmate. The class spent valuable time looking for that workbook. The teacher became more annoyed as we wasted so much time because of my foolishness. The longer the search took, the more I realized I would have to reveal the truth. That revelation would cost me. Humiliation in front of my peers was the penalty for my decision to hide Mike's workbook. I learned a very important lesson about truth telling that day. I never lied again and could not imagine that people would ever think of doing such a thing. Lying to an authority figure was not part of my plans—present, past, or future.

When we arrived at the United States/Canadian border, I realized that even though I always told the truth, the fact that others have lied and gotten away with horrible atrocities as a result of their dishonesty can affect those who do the right thing. The border patrol officer asked me why we were coming to Canada. That was an easy answer. "We're just passing through to visit family in Michigan." "Okay, that was simple," I thought. I was ready to complete the next seven hours of our twelve hour drive. The problem was that although I thought things were complete, the officer did not. The interrogation was about to begin.

"Who are these young men?"

Easy answer again. "Sons."

"Where is their father?"

"He stayed home to work while we are visiting family."

"Do you have certified documentation that he has given you permission to take them through Canada?"

"No, I was just planning to drive through and save a few hours of travel by doing so."

He said that we would have to be detained so that it could be determined if we were running from authorities. I truthfully said, "It's just Canada. Can't we just pass through?"

The border patrol officer was offended, and he let me know. "This is an INTERNATIONAL BORDER, and we must make sure that you are telling the truth."

International Border! How could I forget? Not "just Canada!" What a mess! I wondered how long we would be detained. DETAINED at an INTERNATIONAL BORDER! The five-year old was crying; he wanted to continue on our big journey. The seventeen-old was angry; why couldn't they just take my word? As for me, I was fearful that they were going to put a wanted poster up for me for thinking it was "just Canada."

We completed the detention process with our photographs and

fingerprints taken, all to be scanned for data about fugitives from the law. Unfortunately, this precedent has been set because of people who do not live in truth.

I'm thankful that all ended well. Not only did we have a wonderful adventure, but we also have had many laughs at the idea that I might be wanted for disrespecting Canada.

The beauty of it was I taught the boys that in spite of circumstances, we are to be honest people. However, truth telling is important to God. Being seekers, teachers, and preachers of the truth is commanded by God. The Bible tells us in Proverbs 12:22 "The Lord detests lying lips, but He delights in men who are truthful."

I have since traveled to Canada again without being detained. I am grateful that the most important message from all of this is not just to speak the truth—but to speak the truth in love. The truth is I love Canada!

School Shopping

SOME DAYS JUST SEEM TO be more glorious than others. I don't mean weather-wise. Yes, the sun-filled, humidity free, warm days of a beautiful New England summer are glorious, but I mean those days when the Spirit of God is just engulfing every moment of our lives. You know that praying all the time, washing in God's word kind of day, even with the birds and crickets singing their praise to God.

Well, the reason we can so distinctly recognize that kind of day is because we have also experienced the dark, dreary, rainy, yukky kind of days. You know the kind where it seems everything you hear is annoying, everyone driving around you is inconsiderate, and not one thing goes right kind of day. Why can't every day be a lovely spirit-filled day?

Part of the kind of day you will have starts with how much did you invite God to be part of your day? We need to ask ourselves, "Am I going to try to do my day in my own strength or in God's power?"

I admit I have not always tried to do things in God's way. School shopping has never been a favorite time of year for me. Kids have grown, getting closer to that time they will leave me, even though I know that is what needs to happen. So trying to do a school clothes shopping day with my youngest son as he was preparing to enter his junior year of high school was not going to be a favorite kind of day.

It was a glorious, perfect summer day. But I was a complete moody mess. Having been diagnosed several years before with fibromyalgia had given me many opportunities to surrender to the limitation of what my physical body might or might not be able to do. Today was a struggle day.

This was a flare up day. That meant that my entire body felt as if I had done an entire Iron Man swimming, biking, and running competition and then gone a full ten rounds with whoever the current heavyweight champion of the world was. By the way, I don't know how to ride a bike; I, at best, float in the pool, and I have never understood the need to run unless one of my children was in danger. Boxing—well, my head hurts just thinking of being hit by one of those muscle bound fellows. I'm not muscle bound; maybe more like chubby bound. So, my physical body was a complete pile of pain.

Obviously, my body was not going to work so well to go school shopping. However, the idea of sending my husband and son off to do this ritual without me was more painful than what I felt in my body. Even though my legs and arms were so heavy with pain and I couldn't do the simple things, my sweet husband helped me get up and dress. I assured him that the customer service area of the mall would have a wheelchair I could use.

Every step became a battle, just to get to the car. That was my first goal. Then I found out that my son would be driving. He had received his learner's permit to drive only weeks before; therefore every time that he was going somewhere, in his mind it was a "must" that he drive. Really, even today, the best thing for me to do in a fibromyalgia flare up is to remove stress and to rest. (I am getting stressed just writing about this).

Although it was not a dangerous ride to the mall, it was not exactly stress free for me or my husband. He hates to leave my side, and he realized that he would have to go to the customer service by himself to acquire the wheelchair I would need. He was not happy about it, which was quite evident.

Making the long story short is that we ended up finding some really good bargains for both of my guys. There were lots of clearance racks finds that blessed us all.

Having to be in that wheelchair was very humbling, and I am glad it only happens once in a while now. Two days later I was fine and able to skip into church and up the stairs to do my job for the Lord.

Surrendering to the will of God daily is a victorious way to get through any kind of day. Sunshine or rain will not make it a good day. Allowing the SON of God to shine through is what makes for glorious day.

This Isn't the
Football Field

NOT KNOWING THE COURSE OR direction that our lives will take is often one of the biggest challenges we will face in life. Since becoming a student of the Bible, I am frequently reminded that God uses everything that happens as part of His plan.

That is not to say that everything will always be pleasant to go through or endure, but if we recognize them, there will always be opportunities to build character along the way.

Have you ever had any of those strange "Twilight Zone" moments? You know the ones where you ask yourself, "Did this really just happen?" These are monumental life illustrations of instances that impact our thoughts, our plans, and our direction in life. On my way to a regular craft group that meets once a month, one of these mind-blowing events occurred.

One of the greatest loves I have had in my life is the love of creating crafts of every kind. God is the ultimate Creator, and He has allowed some of us to have a passion for making things. I have enjoyed cross-stitching, beading, crocheting, painting, and paper crafting since I was a young girl. For me there is great joy in creating.

It is exhilarating to learn a new technique. I also enjoy sharing time with other women who share this passion.

Crafting can trace its roots to Eve in the garden. After Adam and Eve sinned, it was necessary to make something to cover themselves so they could hide from God. This quick act of creating something to make us feel better in a moment began there.

We have come a long way since Eve created the first outfits made from leaves. Ladies through the centuries have gathered together to share the lessons they have learned while creating the project they needed. At times these gatherings also provided women an opportunity to have fellowship and gather together to talk about the family news.

On the day of my "Twilight Zone" incident, I had left my house early to arrive on time; 9:00 a.m. was the goal. It was a crisp October morning with bright sunshine and a chill in the air. The new holiday ideas for making Christmas cards and gifts would be the talk of the morning.

I paid no attention to my journey as the drive was very familiar and that meant I could enjoy the ride by myself singing at the top of my lungs—praise, pop, and rock singing sooths my soul! It was a rich spectacular autumn day with falling leaves, apples on the trees, and pumpkins on the porches. My spirit was filled with joy and anticipation.

The best part was that my son had just completed a busy year of baseball. With workouts that had begun in January, for several teams that he played for, including high school Junior Varsity, Babe Ruth, All-Star travel (local), Elite travel (many towns from Canada to Virginia) and fall leagues all running together and overlapping to the point that October was when baseball wrapped up until we started all over again in January. A few weeks of not driving to the next town for the next tournament. Baseball was his game. If he wasn't playing it, he was learning about or talking about it. His passion for baseball rivaled my love of crafting.

I proceeded down the street where our stamp club gathering place was located. I was looking forward to seeing my friends as we would play with papers and punches to create cards to send encouragement to others. It was normal to drive toward the right and then do a U-turn to get parked and go inside to start our fun. At that moment a car pulled up beside me with the passenger window down and the driver yelling something at me. I did an instant replay of my drive over. Had I done something wrong? Did I have something dangling from my car? Why was this person yelling at me?

In order to find out, I realized that I would have to roll my window down and inquire about her situation. Someone I had never met began yelling at me. "This isn't the football field! This can't be the football field! Where is the football field?"

I was ushered to a place of wonder and mystique as I listened to the woman's tale. She began following me almost immediately after I left my home. She had decided since I was leaving so early, I must be headed to the location she desired to find. She told me the reason she had followed me was because of the school football sticker on the back of my car. She made these things up in her head, assuming that I was going to the football field.

Let me explain that the sticker she was talking about was a baseball sticker. My son had played one season of flag football when he was five. That's it; there were no more football events for us. He was now sixteen and baseball was the only game he wanted anything to do with. Baseball fields located on the whole east coast I could find and have found, but not football fields.

Since I had no idea where a football field was, helping this woman was not something that I could do. She had followed me, not having any idea where I was going. It never occurred to me that I was leading someone. As far as I knew, my journey was my own, not a convoy.

How could this happen? What a strange event this turned out to be. I never will know if she found the football field. What impact could this bizarre encounter have on either of our lives? For moments after she pulled away, I sat in my car stunned to think about what had just transpired.

I was yelled at for going on my regular route to my appointed goal and not leading this person to her desired destination. This happened because she wanted to see a football game, and I had a baseball sticker on the back of my car. All I wanted was to peacefully go join my gal pals and craft.

What could all of this mean?" As a teacher I was always looking for illustrations to make my point. This was certainly a doozy for that.

> Lesson # 1 – Who are we following? Why do we blindly go somewhere or do something because someone else is? How can we ever get anywhere if we follow someone who doesn't know the right destination? Communication between the follower and the leader is key.

Lesson #2 - am I a leader worthy of being followed? That day I knew my destination and had the plan all made for which route to take because there were several ways to get there. Doing my planning ahead made me confident in where I was going, but I wasn't prepared for the idea of anyone following me.

Playing follow the leader as children was one thing. We could safely arrive back in the classroom even if our leader wasn't good at directions. However, two vital issues in life require us to think about

(1) Who are we following?
(2) Who is doing the leading?

These are questions we should ask ourselves frequently. Is this friend going where I should go? Will I be setting a bad example if I say or do _____? (We can each fill in the blank). Whether we realize it or not, someone is being the leader in your life. For me that leader will always be the Lord Jesus. The words "He leads me…" begin many Biblical verses. We should be like Joshua and put our trust in God and follow Him. "…But as for me and my household, we will serve the Lord" Joshua 24:15.

I failed at being a leader that day because I wasn't paying attention to the one following me. Be alert to those around you. Help them find their way by sharing Jesus. And it might not hurt to teach them how to plan for the journey on their own as well. For sure, God has given us the greatest map for our lives, His Holy Bible. May you always find the fields you are looking for, whether they be filled with baseballs, footballs, or daisies! The best way to get anywhere is to ask for help. God will help you find your way.

Being a follower of Christ is the most important journey any of us will ever take. The Bible is given to us to help us find our way when we are lost. Please don't get your wisdom from bumper stickers, they might not mean what you think they do!

A Special Day

THE DAILY ROUTINE OF LIFE can often become so busy or mundane that it does not allow our vision to see the blessings all around us. As my children have grown and become parents themselves, it has been my privilege to become more of an observer in their lives, watching them in this role and seeing how they do things so much better than I ever did. I treasure those moments of just gathering the aromas of the lives of my children and grandchildren. I am flooded with blessed emotions as if smelling deeply of God's bouquet of roses.

"Stop and smell the roses" is a familiar phrase told to us in song, in advertisements, and cheap counsel for slowing down a little every day. A rose is truly enjoyed when it is breathed in deeply. The aroma sends thrills of pleasure and delight for most of us though our entire nervous system. In the midst of all that sensory satisfaction of perfume, color, and the softness of the petals, we can forget the hardness of the thorns that protect these gorgeous flowers.

Enjoying time alone individually with my children has become a rare jewel that I find only a few times a year. Whether it is a morning of garage sale perusing with my gifted bargain hunting daughter, an evening of painting a canvas with my creative daughter, or a day in New York City with my look-alike daughter, I treasure them all.

An unusual incident occurred on one of these special occasions in New York City that may cause others to wonder about my blessed life. I, nevertheless, maintain that God has richly blessed me.

Whether walking or riding in a cab in the city on a gorgeous, warm but not humid day, people can experience New York through each of their senses. Although I was in a cab, the smells of the day set the tone for me from the aroma of the wood-fire baked pizza there on the street to the odor of sewer lines being repaired very close to my location. Every sense was awakened, reminding me that I was able to enjoy visiting one of the most unique cities in our world, home of Central Park with its beautiful roses, and horse drawn carriages.

Closing my eyes, I reflected about the past when a cab wasn't yellow with four wheels and honking loudly, but rather the streets were filled with the clip clop of the shoed horses pulling their handsome cabs and the scent of the multitude of those horses that had been on the street in front of and behind us. I would have been dressed in a long layered and ruffled dress with puffed sleeves and a glorious matching hat. Oh, I do love to play dress-up only now it must be in my mind or my family would put me away. A vision of Victorian loveliness… that was me in the back of my slow moving mode of city transportation. Smells, sounds, sights all invigorating my spirit of adventure.

As we rode in the cab along Central Park west, I enjoyed my little fantasy. That was until that sound, that awful sound, interrupted my reverie. With the cab windows down, we could hear, smell, and see everything around us. At the moment of that sound, I could only imagine what every conversation was about. When that distinct plop occurred, I was sure someone had thrown a hateful glob my way. However, I instantly realized that this plop had come from heavenward.

Yes, it happened. While riding in a cab, with the windows only slightly down I was pooped on by a pigeon. What kind of amazing physics had to take place for that to actually happen? The speed of the car and the bird, the angle of the window it fell through in combination with the trajectory, gravitational acceleration and timing. Incredible!

My laughter in the back of the cab was uncontained and it quickly spread to my daughter as I told her what had taken place. It was the funniest thing that could happen in a cab in NYC. Thankfully, I did have a napkin so that I could wipe this very large pigeon's digested lunch off of my lap, hand, and the car door it had come to rest upon. My daughter's friend that was with us did not find it as amusing as we did!! She was just glad it hadn't happened to her because it would have "ruined her day" was her statement of the situation.

I suppose I could have been mad at the cab driver for my window being just a bit open. I imagine being mad at the pigeon would do no good. So, why not be disgusted with City Hall for allowing pigeons to be there, which means finally I could have decided to be angry at God for creating pigeons.

Ultimately, I thanked God for the entire event because I was chosen to bring laughter to others through something that had happened to me. I didn't look or smell like a rose, but God used me to bring joy to others that day. Laughter is a gift from GOD! I am blessed! Life greatest joys are often a result of how we choose to respond to the mundane issues of daily living.

Printed in the United States
by Baker & Taylor Publisher Services